Love *God*

~~porn~~

WHO'S GETTING YOUR HEART, SOUL, MIND & STRENGTH?

AARON REYNOLDS
FOREWORD BY CHRISTOPHER D. HUDSON

EPIGRAPH

"Pornography, by its very nature, is an equal opportunity toxin. It damages the viewer, the performer, and the spouses and the children of the viewers and the performers. It is toxic miseducation about sex and relationships. It is more toxic the more you consume, the 'harder' the variety you consume and the younger and more vulnerable the consumer."
DR. MARY ANNE LAYDEN

Contents

SECTION 1: HEART

SECTION 2: SOUL

SECTION 3: MIND

SECTION 4: STRENGTH

ACTION PLAN

FOREWORD

*"Love the Lord Your God with all
your heart, soul, mind, and strength."*
—JESUS

Pornography.

It's a tool of the enemy that attacks the very core
of Jesus' Great Commandment. It's one activity that
erodes a Christian's ability to love God with their heart,
soul, mind, and strength.

Porn attacks our *heart* and erodes our values that
once aligned with those of Jesus.

Porn attacks our *soul* and squeezes out intimacy
with God.

Porn attacks our *mind* and damages the ability to
focus and think clearly.

Porn attacks our *strength* and steals the ability to
perform life's tasks at the highest level.

In a brilliant move, Satan has inspired one vice that
has devasting consequences. This single temptation is
able to strike at the very areas that damage our intimacy with God.

As a result we have brothers and sisters who:

- ❖ Live with guilt. The effect is that they don't engage with others or serve others.
- ❖ Suffer in shame. Because of the darkness within them they lose their ability to grow and enjoy relationships with God and others.
- ❖ Fear exposure. They hide in their relationships.

Men and women who should be building into others, serving, and encouraging are cowering in corners, excusing their lack of intimacy, suffering in silence, and doubting their faith as they give in to cycles of guilt, fear, and shame.

This is not a young person's problem. This is not a young man's problem. This is a problem that is gutting the church. It afflicts men and women, young and old.

This book is arranged around the four areas that Jesus urged to be reserved for God—heart, soul, mind, and strength—and shows how porn undermines each area. The book also includes a short study guide that can be used by accountability partners or small groups as well as some practical ideas for dealing with this pervasive problem.

This book is challenging. Share a copy with a friend and discuss it together. The conversations you have may change your lives.

Christopher D. Hudson
ReadEngageApply.com

HEART

Above all else, guard your heart,
for everything you do flows from it.
(PROVERBS 4:23)

A HEARTY POISON

The human heart is no bigger than your fist, yet every day it beats around 100,000 times and sends 2,000 gallons of blood throughout the body. The heart can even continue beating after it is disconnected from the rest of the body.

Like the rest of God's most prized creation, the heart is an incredible wonder. While we rely on the physical heart to sustain and enhance our physical lives, we also rely on the spiritual heart to sustain our spiritual growth and health. In both cases, however, the heart is vulnerable to exploitation and corruption.

God intended for human beings to be loved. This affection is often demonstrated in relationships through touching, holding, kissing, and sexual intimacy. When those feelings are neglected, however, it is scientifically proven that both the human heart and body suffers.

People who are deprived of human affection literally grow sickly. Their physical and mental development is stunted. This can create a longing so profound that humans will desperately search for expressions of affection through other means.

Pornography has become a misguided substitute in this area because it tricks men and women into believing it adequately replaces affection.

Pornography does not make you a better lover, or even better at sex. In fact, it does the exact opposite. Porn reinforces isolation, neglect, depression, and loneliness. God never intended for humans, who are His most prized and beloved creations, to experience these conditions.

Porn is a deadly poison to the heart.

NOT ENOUGH SEX

The real problem with pornography is not that it offers *too much* sex but instead that it offers *not enough*. Porn cannot replace the intense desire and emotion that are found in true intimacy.

Pornography is everywhere on the internet, yet its depictions of sex and its portrayal of the roles of men and women are extremely inaccurate.

Perhaps you already know this, but do you really *understand* it?

Among the biggest temptations related to pornography is not the physical attraction it offers but rather the emotional numbness it temporarily provides.

People seek porn because of the cheap thrill and fantasy it gives them in contrast to the lasting, intimate emotions found in a real relationship. Porn trains the heart to substitute lust for love, forcing the heart to seek intimacy by artificial means.

This is like confusing a mannequin with a human body. While they both have similar features and provide for the display of clothing, one is very real and one is obviously fake.

In the same way, porn is a poor imitation of the real thing.

Pornography trains the heart to prefer *viewing* rather than *interacting*.

A PRICE TO PAY

Which sandwich would you prefer? The first is already made with no option to change anything. It might address your hunger, but there might be things about it you don't like. The second is custom made—you pick your bread, meats, cheeses, condiments, and vegetables. "I'll take more mayo and less tomato." The possibilities are endless.

The adult "entertainment" industry has constructed a world that customizes and personalizes porn down to the very last detail. Its wealth of online content has allowed viewers to select exactly who and what they want to see, tailored to the finest detail.

This essentially reduces women to objects men can selfishly manipulate to create their own version of the perfect woman.

But what is perfection? Is it really the woman in the video who looks more attractive than your wife? Is it really the woman that single men envision as their next girlfriend?

The endless options in pornography fit perfectly in

today's on-demand, abundance-in-variety-and-selection
society.

But how does this impact women and our percep-
tion of what makes a female beautiful?

From the Book of Genesis we learn that humankind
was created in the image of God. As His image-bearers,
God designed us to reflect His holy attributes of love,
joy, peace, patience, kindness, goodness, faithfulness,
gentleness, and self-control.[1]

Pornography, however, encourages and promotes
the "worship" of women instead of God, effectively
asking women to provide something only God can
provide: GENUINE love, affection, and validation.

In John 13:35, Jesus makes this simple statement,
"This is how everyone will recognize that you are my
disciples—when they see the love you have for each
other."

True love is others-focused, not self-focused. The
person who loves as Jesus indicated seeks the best for
the person who is loved.

Do we really love women when we view porn?

**Porn always costs someone; generally
women pay the highest price.**

---

[1]   Galatians 5:22–23

FANTASY OR REALITY?

Children often create imaginary worlds. Anyone who has ever watched a child entertain him- or herself for hours with nothing more than a box or stick can understand the profound nature of fantasy.

Later in life kids turn to video games and movies to get the same effect. These fantasies, however, are intended to be an escape from reality. They are not designed to replace it.

But they do.

A writer for *New York Magazine* once summarized, "Today's real naked women are just bad porn."[2]

It is true. Pornography is not an escape from reality but rather a replacement for it. We no longer regard real women as actual representations of beauty. Instead, we substitute them with porn actresses—something artificial and fake.

This leads to what Gary Brooks calls the disorder

---

[2]   Naomi Wolf, "The Porn Myth," *New York Magazine*, http://nymag.com/nymetro/news/trends/n_9437.

of validation.[3] In this condition a guy gauges how much of a "man" he is based on the degree of beauty he sees in the women he is with. Thus men with average looking girlfriends are not nearly as manly as those with centerfold models.

Of course this is an absurd concept, yet it is exactly how society teaches us to regard not only the beauty of a woman but also the masculinity of a man. Porn attempts to validate the man as much as the woman, but it's wrong in both respects.

Pornography trains men to see fewer women as "porn-worthy."

---

[3]   Gary R. Brooks, *The Centerfold Syndrome: How Men Can Overcome Objectification and Achieve Intimacy with Women* (San Francisco: Jossy-Bass Publications, 1995).

SLOW, STEADY DESTRUCTION

The termite is one of the smallest creatures on the earth. While there are many species of the insect, most are less than an inch long. Despite their small size, they have a big impact. They can work 24 hours a day, seven days a week eating wood and paper. Because they work silently and in dark areas, often their activity goes unnoticed until it's too late. Unless people are diligent to inspect regularly for termites and to treat their activity when it's discovered, termites can create major damage to a structure. It's estimated that every year they cause over $5 billion in damage.

In many ways, pornography acts like termites in our hearts. A redeemed heart initially pursues God and His ways, but over time any heart can be attacked by porn, which is always available and seeking an unwitting host. Without regular inspection and intervention, our tender hearts can quickly suffer from the devastating and costly effects of porn.

The Bible reminds us that a tender heart[4] is:

❖ Sensitive
❖ Pliable
❖ Yielding

Pornography doesn't contribute to a sensitive, yielding heart. Instead, it creates a breeding ground for destruction.

Your physical heart can be strengthened or it can be weakened. The same is true for your spiritual heart. It is at its most pure form when you come into a relationship with Christ. Over time, however, it is threatened and corrupted by sin. The more sin in your life, the more it restricts God's true intentions for your heart and for your life.

**Pornography slowly eats away
at a tender heart for God.**

---

[4]   https://biblehub.com/sermons/auth/sibbes/the_tender_heart.htm

DIGITAL VOYEURISM

What would a world be like if every single item in it were fraudulent? In such a world, the house you lived in, the food you ate, and the car you drove would all be a sham.

In many ways such a world already exists.

Most people enjoy eating food rather than watching others eat. The same is true for the mutually comforting, gratifying, and enjoyable activity of sex.

Yet we live in an era of digital voyeurism where many men and women get more pleasure from watching others engage in sexual activity than from personally engaging in it.

Tragically, our fixation with voyeurism has ignited a toxic culture with many misconceptions about sex, especially among those under the age of 35.

An inverse relationship exists between the amount of pornography viewed and one's overall sexual satisfaction. A study of college-age students related to the harms of pornography confirms this finding.[5]

---

[5] Dolf Zillmann and Jennings Bryant, "Effects of massive exposure

Over a six-week period, participants in the study were shown various amounts of porn. The group exposed to the most pornography was far more prone to demonstrate less satisfaction with their intimate partner, including their partner's "physical appearance, affection and sexual performance."

The study researchers concluded, "Consumers eventually compare appearance and performance of pornographic models with that of their intimate partners, and this comparison rarely favors their intimate partners."

Pornography distorts reality; we believe it's something that it's not.

---

to pornography," in *Pornography and Sexual Aggression* (New York: Academic Press, 1984). Dolf Zillmann and Jennings Bryant, "Shifting preferences in pornography consumption," *Communication Research* 13 (1986), 560–578. Dolf Zillmann and Jennings Bryant, "Pornography's impact on sexual satisfaction," *Journal of Applied Social Psychology* 18 (1988), 438–453. Dolf Zillmann and Jennings Bryant, "Effects of Prolonged Consumption of Pornography on Family Values," *Journal of Family Issues* 9 (1988), 518–544.

A SWIPING GENERATION

The concept is simple. After the photo loads on the screen you swipe right if you find the person attractive; swipe left if the person is unattractive to you.

Modern dating apps have created a method of rating men and women without the pain and discomfort of doing it in person. There is no need to tell a person that you don't find them attractive. The app does it for you.

What kind of impact does this have on your brain? What impact does it have on your heart?

Our world can get polluted very quickly. It can be difficult to discover anything truly beautiful among the muck. In our digital age, however, instead of venturing into the smog to find beauty on their own, many people prefer to sit in front of a screen for a false representation of beauty to be presented to them.

Pornography completely alters our understanding of beauty. In this world, everything has a number attached to it. Men rate every *single* feature of the female body. The woman's height, weight, hair color, breast size, waistline, and legs are all closely examined and criti-cized. The same is true for women who rate men on their physical characteristics. Only a *perfect* figure is passable.

True beauty in this world, however, is found in being made in the image of God. Scripture tells us that after God finished creating humans in His own image, He rested from His creative work. God saw everything that He had made and it was "very good."[6] No other imitations of beauty were necessary.

Porn causes people to play God, undermining His definition of beauty.

---

[6]   Genesis 1:27–31

SPIRITUAL TOOLBOX

A hammer's head, not its handle, is designed to drive in a nail. A Phillips screwdriver does no good on a flat head screw. A drill won't help when you need to cut a piece of wood. All of these tools are effective, but only when used properly.

The same is true of sex. Sex serves many practical applications. At its most physical level, sex enables humans to reproduce. Yet when used as God designed it, sex also generates feelings of intimacy, companionship, and physical pleasure.[7] One could then conclude that sex is remarkably spiritual.

So what happens when it is not?

Pornography is a prime example of sex offered at a physical level with little or no emotional or spiritual connection. Men and women turn to porn because they feel insignificant, lonely, isolated, incompetent, or depressed. These negative feelings can be driven by a number of factors, including:

[7] https://carm.org/biblical-purpose-of-sex

- ❖ Fear
- ❖ Emotional wounds
- ❖ Resentment
- ❖ Trauma

You can't address a problem and make the necessary repairs by using the wrong tools. Spiritual problems require a spiritual solution.

Pornography is the result of seeking a *physical* solution to a *spiritual* problem.

STEPPIN' ON MY SNEAKERS

Your new shoes cost a lot, so you're protective of them. If someone steps on them and then apologizes, you'll brush it off as an accident. It's different, however, if someone stomps your shoes again and again. No one deliberately steps on another person's toes unless they want to start a fight. That person is selfish, thinking only of themselves. Unfortunately, this happens not only with shoes but also in important areas of life.

The Big Book of Alcoholics Anonymous notes that selfishness is "the root of our troubles" and is "driven by a hundred forms of fear, self-delusion, self-seeking, and self-pity [where] we step on the toes of our fellows, and they retaliate."[8]

Selfishness may not be the intention of an addict, but it's a result of addiction. Addiction causes people to hurt others and many of those who are hurt will cause hurt in return.

Pornography is addictive, thus it breeds selfishness that creates widespread problems. More than

---

[8] "The Big Book of Alcoholics Anonymous," 62.

one heart can be broken because of the addiction of porn.

When asked about the greatest commandment, Jesus responded: "Love the Lord your God with all your *heart* and with all your *soul* and with all your *mind* and with all your *strength*. The second is this: 'Love your neighbor as yourself.' There is no commandment greater than these."[9]

Can a broken heart still love God with all its strength? When the heart becomes tainted by selfishness, does it still love a neighbor as much as it loves itself?

In 1 Corinthians 13:4–8, the Apostle Paul notes that love:

- ❖ Is patient
- ❖ Is kind
- ❖ Does not envy
- ❖ Does not boast
- ❖ Is not proud
- ❖ Does not dishonor
- ❖ Is not self-seeking

What problems is selfishness causing in your life? How is your selfishness impacting others?

Pornography makes the heart selfish and hurts others in the process.

---

[9]   Mark 12:29–31, emphasis added

YOU ARE NOT WORTHY!

A man stood outside the church draped in a giant rosary for being late. A criminal was shackled to a pillory for a petty offense and had to endure public insult. The adulteress was forced to wear a scarlet "A" on her gown when in the town square.

The history of the world includes examples of public humiliation and shaming. In the United States, this was a common punishment until the 20th century. While still used in other parts of the world, public humiliation is highly ineffective at making a person "learn their lesson."

Some people support shaming those who are involved with pornography. Typically, however, this only forces victims to retreat. Others argue that if people (such as those in the church) simply stopped shaming porn users then its negative consequences would be eliminated. Their premise is that if the shame stops, porn users will stop hating themselves for the so-called negative effects of porn.

This is a delicate issue, especially for churches. Do we confront it with a harsh, direct approach or do we take a more sensitive, understanding approach?

Dr. Brene Brown, a leading researcher on shame, growth, and change has noted that in order to enact change one must first understand the difference between shame and guilt.[10] They are not the same.

❖ Brown says that **guilt** is "adaptive and helpful." In her opinion, guilt comes when we regard something we have done (or failed to do) that is against our personal values. Guilt creates discomfort and motivation to change. A guilty party thinks, "This behavior is bad. I should change."

❖ **Shame** compounds guilt into making individuals believe they are inherently flawed, unworthy of love, and thus incapable of change. While guilt can motivate change in a positive way, shame reinforces negative thoughts and leads to more self-destruction. A shameful party laments: "I am a bad person. I probably will never change."

Shame contributes to addiction and other erratic behaviors.[11] Instead of reinforcing the need to take control and change our lives, it involves rejection and further neglect. Shame is counterproductive.

We must love victims of porn addiction rather than

---

[10]   Brene Brown, "Shame v. Guilt" (January 14, 2013). https://brenebrown.com/blog/2013/01/14/shame-v-guilt/

[11]   Randy Gilliland, Mikle South, Bruce N. Carpenter, & Sam A. Hardy, "The Roles of Shame and Guilt in Hypersexual Behavior," in *Sexual Addiction & Compulsivity, The Journal of Treatment & Prevention,* Vol. 18 (2011), 12–29. http://dx.doi.org/10.1080/107 20162.2011.551182

shaming them. No one is as bad as the worst thing they do. Shame directly attacks the tender hearts God desires for us, whether we are the victims or the "judges."

> **Those who struggle with porn can't overcome it by living in shame.**

SOUL

*What good will it be for someone
to gain the whole world, yet forfeit
their soul? Or what can anyone
give in exchange for their soul?*
(MATTHEW 16:26)

INWARD AND OUTWARD

Jesus said some damning things about lust.

In his famous Sermon on the Mount, Jesus said, "anyone who looks at a woman lustfully has already committed adultery with her in his heart."[12]

This is an extremely profound statement, because Jesus recognized adultery not only as a physical action (one's strength) but also an action involving the heart, soul, and mind.[13]

Jesus summarized that if "your right eye causes you to stumble, gouge it out and throw it away" because "it is better for you to lose one part of your body than for your whole body to be thrown into hell."[14]

Jesus may be remarkably direct with His thoughts on lust, but His words were carefully selected for a purpose.

Lust attacks the mind, then assaults the heart, strength, and soul.

[12] Matthew 5:27
[13] Mark 12:30
[14] Matthew 5:29

HALF A MILLION YEARS

Why is it difficult to focus on even the most trivial tasks? For instance, when we start to pray, why do our minds often wander elsewhere . . . sometimes even to porn?

Pornography is being viewed at unprecedented levels. In 2015, 4.3 billion hours of pornography were watched on a *single* website.[15] That's the equivalent of half a million years. Sadly, all of this time is spent on an activity that causes great contamination and harm to our society.

Have you ever been to a big city with pollution so bad there was a permanent cloud that hovered over the city? Pornography does the same to our souls.

It's with good reason that so many in the church lament over people's lack of focus, especially related to prayer. This is especially troubling because prayer is one of the most important things a Christian can do. It is a divine time, personally reserved to communicate with God and nurture our relationship with Him. We will never experience the fullness of

---

[15] https://fightthenewdrug.org/overview/#world

life God desires for us when we allow something else, like porn, to distract us and erode our sacred time with Him.

Pornography impairs our focus and inhibits our prayers.

DRIVE-THRU CHURCH

Why do consumers enjoy a fast food drive-thru? It's quick, comfortable, and convenient. Without leaving their car, people can can pull up, order, pay, get their food, and be off to more important things.

In many ways the church in our time is like a drive-thru. Too many believers pull in for an hour (on an occasional Sunday) then head off to more important things (old habits) the rest of the week.

In March 2005, *Christianity Today* published the results of a study called "Christians and Sex." Out of 680 pastors surveyed, 57 percent said addiction to pornography was the *most* damaging issue to their congregation.

Pornography is not just an issue with the "secular crowd." One study reports that 50 percent of all Christian men and 20 percent of all Christian women are addicted to pornography.[16] That's one in two Christian men and one in five Christian women!

---

[16] ChristiaNet, Inc., "ChristiaNet poll finds that evangelicals are addicted to porn," *Marketwire*, Aug. 7, 2006. http://www.marketwire.com/press-release/christianet-poll-finds-that-evangelicals-are-addicted-to-porn-703951.htm (accessed Dec. 27, 2012).

Another study[17] found that the majority of Christian men between 18–30 years old are involved with pornography in some way:

- ❖ 77 percent admitted they look at porn at least monthly
- ❖ 36 percent view pornography on a daily basis
- ❖ 32 percent admit being addicted to pornography
- ❖ 12 percent believe they may be addicted to pornography

Porn use isn't just limited to the people in the pews. Yet another study found that 33 percent of clergy admitted they have visited a sexually explicit website, with 18 percent confirming they visited explicit websites between "a couple of times a month" and "more than once a week."[18]

These numbers are cited not to bash the church, but to explain exactly how common the issue is within Christianity. As one individual put it, "If you think you can't fall into sexual sin, then you're godlier than David, stronger than Samson, and wiser than Solomon."[19]

---

[17] http://www.charismanews.com/us/45671-shocker-study-shows -most-christian-men-are-into-porn
[18] Christine J. Gardner, "Tangled in the worst of the web: What Internet porn did to one pastor, his wife, his ministry, their life," *Christianity Today*, March 5, 2001. http://www.christianitytoday. com/ct/2001/march5/1.42.html?paging=off (accessed Dec. 27, 2012).
[19] Leadership Journal, "The leadership survey on pastors and internet pornography," *Christianity Today*, Jan. 1, 2001. http:// www.christianitytoday.com/le/2001/winter/12.89.html (accessed Dec. 27, 2012).

So what will the church do about it? Will we continue to sweep the issue under the rug? Will we continue to oppress believers into thinking they are alone, and that "good" Christians don't struggle with pornography?

The early church was a place of deep, personal relationships, conversation, fellowship, and worship. It was the opposite of our drive-thru church culture. As Jesus' followers, we will only overcome the obstacle of pornography when we deal with it directly and honestly.

A drive-thru church can't combat the pervasive nature of pornography.

SOUL SOFTWARE

Not long after the Internet became widely used, antivirus programs were created to help protect computers from cyber-attacks and vulnerabilities. This software has protected countless computers from harm and has helped restore many others that were infected after an attack.

Like a computer, the human body needs its own form of antivirus. We are attacked and constantly threatened by sin. Due to the prevalence of technology, pornography is a relentless source of temptation.

Pornography has existed throughout most of human history. First introduced in rock carvings and pottery paintings, it expanded as photography fueled its availability in magazines and motion pictures. Through the Internet, porn became available 24/7 and smartphones offered accessibility almost anywhere.

While people in ancient times didn't know about internet porn, many societies were saturated with sex. In Corinth, for example, sex was a part of the pagan religions in that region; the temple to Aphrodite was headquarters to thousands of prostitutes who "aided" worshippers on a daily basis.

The Apostle Paul knew the threat of sexual immorality, which is why he wrote to the Christians in Corinth and compared their souls to glue.[20] Paul knew that images have a profound effect on people—they are branded into the mind and initiate feelings in the soul. These images and feelings can lead us into sin if we ignore Paul's warning to "flee from sexual immorality."[21] Only when we allow God's Word and His Spirit to be our antivirus can we be protected from harm and restored from sin.

What are you immersing yourself in on a daily basis—is it pornography or the pursuit of intimacy with God?

Pornography's images are impressionable; they stick to a soul like glue.

---

[20]   1 Corinthians 6:16-19
[21]   1 Corinthians 6:18

RENOVATION AND RESTORATION

Most of us have seen TV shows where an old home is remodeled. The inside is gutted and repairs are made. Cabinets, doors, floors, and walls are replaced. The exterior is repainted and the roof replaced. It's amazing how something old and rundown can be rejuvenated so that it looks new again.

Over time, however, the paint begins to fade and the interior experiences similar wear and tear. These things are expected. Still, if a leak or other issue develops but isn't addressed, there can be greater problems than the house originally experienced.

Becoming a born-again Christian is very much like an old house that gets remodeled. The initial change can be astounding, but the newness gives way to wear and tear. When a problem (like porn use) develops and isn't addressed, however, it can gain a foothold that has a devastating effect on the whole body.

Pornography is an addiction that's a monster to overcome. The best place to start in fighting this addiction is before it gains a foothold, but even when it takes hold we have a weapon. The Apostle Paul challenged us to fill our minds with things that are pure and holy.[22] He said it is impossible to overcome darkness without these right thoughts. Paul acknowledged that recovery can only begin by restoring our relationship with Christ again.

Pure and holy thoughts combat the devastation porn seeks to inflict.

---

[22] Philippians 4:8

HIDDEN IN THE CLOSET

Closets serve as extra storage space for items you don't use very often. Because they aren't accessed as much as other rooms, they can get disorganized. Thus some people avoid opening certain closet doors because they don't want to deal with the clutter.

The same can be true in our lives. Pornography trains men and women to live in a closed closet rather than in the open areas of the house like a kitchen or living room.[23] People trapped by porn hide their actions from others in the household because they don't want to face the demons of guilt and shame.[24]

Shame and guilt are two of our biggest spiritual enemies, but they are not from God. Adam and Eve lived in eternal peace and bliss until they ate from the forbidden tree. As a result, they (along with every other

---

[23] https://fightthenewdrug.org/porn-can-make-you-more-depressed-and-lonely/

[24] An excellent reading on this subject is "My Heart, Christ's Home," by Robert Boyd Munger, http://www.northshorefamily.org/Websites/newproject/images/My_Heart_Christs_Home.pdf

human yet to come) were forever subjected to feeling disgraced from their sin.

Sin in a life can produce self-conscious thoughts that something is wrong or isn't quite right. This not only applies specifically in the area of faith but also relates more generally to morality.

> **Porn enhances fear and anxiety because God is trying to get your attention that something is not right in your life.**

SERVING TWO MASTERS

In ancient times the best shields were constructed of metal to be impenetrable. Yet as a solider took a constant beating, the shield that protected him began to lower. As his strength failed, he could no longer hold up the impenetrable shield. Consequently, he became vulnerable to an attack.

Michael Leahy, a recovering sex addict and author, speaks often at college campuses. He has noted the number one question he is asked: "Can I look at porn recreationally without becoming addicted to it?"

Leahy responds, "Do you think it's okay if I beat and berate my wife just once a month? I'm not addicted to it."[25]

The biggest misunderstanding about pornography, especially with younger generations, is that they do not consider it a significant problem. Some even doubt that it's possible to be addicted to porn.

---

[25] Covenant Eyes official website, "Be Aware: Porn Harms — Is Porn Addictive?" Interview with Michael Leahy, Jan Meza, and Noel Bouche on Covenant Eyes Radio, Episode 106, http://www.covenanteyes. com/2011/07/11/be-aware-porn-harms-is-porn-addictive (accessed November 18, 2011).

Numerous studies and research have dispelled this myth. Pornography is most certainly addictive, and it does destroy lives.[26]

The first significant dent it makes in your spiritual armor is the love and attention it seeks, pulling you away from God. The Bible emphasizes that it is impossible to serve two masters.[27]

The enemy uses the weapon of porn because he knows it distracts our time with the Lord. When we try to maintain both relationships (with porn and with God), in a sense it's like we are trying to fight for two sides in a war. Not only is this fight futile, but it results in casualties on every side.

> **Christians addicted to porn try to serve two masters, thus they can't love God wholeheartedly.**

---

[26] Peter D. Goldberg, Brennan D. Peterson, Karen H. Rosen, and Mary Linda Sara, "Cybersex: The Impact of a Contemporary Problem on the Practices of Marriage and Family Therapists," *Journal of Marital and Family Therapy*, vol.34, issue 4, 2008.

[27] Matthew 6:24

A NARROW PERSPECTIVE

Have you ever gazed through the lens of a telescope? While a telescope enhances your view, it is also highly centralized. You can only focus on a single item. Meanwhile, if you take your eyes away from the lens you can see *all* of the scenery and get the big picture.

Porn addiction is like living a life where you can't remove yourself from the view provided by the telescope. It becomes singular; your outlook is based on an isolated aspect.

Addiction is detrimental not only to your body and mind, but also to your personal relationship with the Lord. The enemy wants porn addiction to attack this relationship more than anything—he wants your perspective to be so narrow that God is removed from view.

The Bible is clear when it describes the relationship God wants with us. Jesus says in Revelation 3:20 that He "stands at the door and knocks." He wants to have an active, not passive, relationship with people.

The Bible also emphasizes the profound nature of sin, and the reality that all of humanity falls victim to it.[28] Our sin keeps us from having a right relationship with God and there's nothing we can do about it. That's the bad news. The good news, however, is that God could and did do something about our sin. He allowed Jesus to die in our place so we could have a right relationship with Him.

Porn addiction keeps us from experiencing everything that comes with a growing relationship with the Lord: joy, peace, hope, and much more. Porn provides a false satisfaction, at least for a while. Of all its disastrous consequences, by far the most tragic is that users rarely get much satisfaction in the latter stages of addiction. By that time, however, their view is so narrow they feel powerless to see clearly again—they think they can never experience the life God wants for them.

Is there any hope? Is there any help? Yes, through the power of God's Spirit our vision can be renewed and restored; we can be released from the devastating effects of porn addiction.

This requires a willingness on our part to change, to do what it takes to get help for our addiction, and, most importantly, to refocus on God and to prioritize His will above our own.

An addiction to pornography narrows our perspective so that God is almost removed from view.

---

[28] Ephesians 2:1; Romans 3:23; 5:12

WHITE-KNUCKLE DRIVING

Many of us have been in a situation while driving that created great tension and intense concern. Perhaps it was a time when you had a close call, barely avoiding an accident. Or maybe you had to continue driving during a serious thunderstorm or snowstorm. We refer to these instances as "white-knuckle driving" because of our tendency to grip the steering wheel so tightly our knuckles turn white.

Now imagine living a life so intense that you feel like you're in a constant state of white-knuckling it. This sounds horrible, right? It is horrible, and that's what it's like for addicts trying to recover from porn addiction on their own. They are in a frequent state of worry and dread because they are trying to go it alone.

If you knew someone struggling with alcoholism you might be quick to suggest that they attend an AA meeting. That organization is well-known even for those who don't struggle with alcohol addiction. Yet with pornography, it seems like society has put a cloak around it or doesn't fully understand its destructive nature and addictive qualities.

While Celebrate Recovery, a Christian-based program, does include support for sex and porn addicts, for the most part we don't hear many people raising awareness about the issue or even recommending treatment options.

This is a concern, especially since addiction is considered a "chronic disease." This means that the disease is not only long-lasting, but also can never be fully cured, just controlled.

Will power to overcome porn addiction just won't cut it.

"The more one uses pornography, the more lonely one becomes," noted a psychologist who has worked with porn addicts for the last 30 years.[29] "Any time [a person] spends much time with the usual pornography usage cycle, it can't help but be a depressing, demeaning, self-loathing kind of experience."[30]

Men are generally not open to discussing deep, personal matters with others, especially related to their habit of pornography. But a conversation *must* be initiated. It's the first step forward.

Porn's intention is to keep users isolated, where they don't seek help from others but do retreat to the comforts of more porn.

---

[29] G. R. Brooks, *The Centerfold Syndrome: How Men Can Overcome Objectification And Achieve Intimacy With Women* (San Francisco: Bass, 1995). Cited In V. C. Yoder, T. B. Virden, & K. Amin, Internet Pornography And Loneliness: An Association? *Sexual Addiction And Compulsivity*, Vol. 12 (2005) 19–44. Doi:10.1080/10720160590933653

[30] Interview with Dr. Gary Brooks, Oct. 23, 2013.

A CRUMBLING FAÇADE

Prior to the 1936 Olympics in Berlin, in an effort to "clean up the city," Adolf Hitler attempted to sweep out "undesirables" known as Romani (Gypsies). While this was disgraceful, people from other countries who attended the Olympic Games were oblivious to those actions and frequently made positive comments about the presentation and overall cleanliness of Berlin.

While it is a stretch to compare pornography to Nazi Germany, there is a correlation between how both attempt to cover up or distract bystanders from the issue at hand.

Pastors agree that one of the biggest issues facing the church today relates to porn and sexuality. Despite this acknowledgement, most pastors admit that they don't feel "very qualified" to address many of these serious issues.[31] Compounding this issue, most men in the church fear admitting an attachment to pornography because they think other Christians do not struggle with it.

---

[31] https://www.christianpost.com/news/most-pastors-dont-feel-qualified-to-address-touchy-sexual-issues-abuse-in-church-survey.html

We live in a church culture where followers are scared to bring up the issue and pastors are hesitant to confront it. Thus nothing gets addressed or resolved.

An executive of an adult video production company once summarized, "Porn doesn't have a demographic–it goes across all demographics."[32]

Like other forms of addiction there is no personal bias or discrimination. All sectors of a community are affected, including the church.

Therefore we *must* answer these two questions:

- ❖ Will believers continue to put up a façade in which everything appears perfectly fine?
- ❖ Will the church get its hands dirty and address the issue of pornography?

Pornography has created a divided church that avoids dealing with one of its biggest issues.

---

[32] Rich Frank, "Naked Capitalists: There's no Business like Porn Business," *New York Times,* May 20, 2001. http://www.nytimes.com/2001/05/20/ magazine/20PORN.html.

SECTION 3:

MIND

*Do not conform to the pattern of
this world, but be transformed by the
renewing of your mind. Then you will be
able to test and approve what God's will
is—his good, pleasing and perfect will.*
(ROMANS 12:2)

NOT ADDICTED

One of the biggest controversies surrounding pornography is whether it leads to addiction.

Some argue that porn is nothing more than a compulsion, a harmless activity for men with a high sex drive. A number of studies[33] through the last two decades, however, strongly argue that viewing pornography is indeed highly addictive.

Watching pornography releases high doses of dopamine in the brain. This chemical creates a rush of pleasure that causes men and women to continue and seek its euphoria by engaging in more porn.

Among the most common characteristics of an addiction is when the substance "interferes with normal daily behavior" and has a "negative impact on some aspect of your life."[34]

Pornography, like alcoholism, is an addiction because soon enough it takes control of a person's life.

---

[33] https://www.yourbrainonporn.com/relevant-research-and-articles-about-the-studies/brain-studies-on-porn-users-sex-addicts/#brain
[34] https://www.psychguides.com/guides/porn-addiction/

The addiction can reveal itself in something as basic as increased tardiness or lower grades at school because porn takes away focus and time from studying. The addiction can progress to something as life-altering as a job loss or problems in a marriage.

There is no value arguing which aspect of a person's life is impacted more severely. The truth is that porn is an "equal opportunity victimizer"—it has a negative impact on every part of life.

Porn is an addiction that destroys lives.

THE SEDUCTIVE MALADY

Is addiction a disease?

This question has been hotly debated for years, though recent conversations are beginning to establish more sympathy for the addicted. While some still view addiction as a choice, scientific evidence confirms the conclusions that in its mid-to-later stages, addiction fundamentally changes the brain and the body.

Consequently, addiction is now defined as a disease by most medical associations, including the American Medical Association and the American Society of Addiction Medicine.[35]

Like cancer, diabetes, and heart disease, addiction is caused by a combination of behavioral, environmental, and biological factors (including genetics) that make some people more prone to it.

It is unfair to paint porn addiction as simply a choice. Yes, in the early stages an individual *decides* to look at pornography, which is a poor decision. It's

---

[35] https://www.centeronaddiction.org/what-addiction/addiction-disease

no different, however, from the poor decisions many people made earlier in life related to diet and exercise—choices that have now contributed to their diabetes or heart disease.

The Center on Addiction reports that 25 to 50 percent of people with a substance use problem have a severe, chronic disorder. Since pornography addiction is not fully curable, extensive treatment and peer support is necessary to overcome its evils and to help people avoid relapse.

It's time we started a conversation on the dangers of pornography. It's time we began to treat it like an addiction comparable to alcoholism and drug abuse. The church can and should become a leader on this subject.

We will only begin to help those with pornography addiction after we *acknowledge* it as a disease.

STAR OF THE SHOW

Though most men turn to pornography because they are aroused by the female they see in a video, men also become enamored with porn because of the role they play in it.

The brain naturally imagines itself as being involved in pornography, where the viewer is no longer a member of the audience but instead is the star of the show.[36] This is similar to watching a traditional film, where you may gravitate to the story because you can see a part of yourself in the main character.

An overwhelming number of studies have noted that pornography is more than just a harmless compulsion; studies have frequently concluded that pornography is not simply the body's response but also the brain's response.

A man's heightened arousal occurs not only from a naked woman, but also from the role he assumes, which makes him feel sexy.

---

[36] https://www.covenanteyes.com/2015/07/31/4-ways-porn-warps -the-male-brain/

Do you think pornography is harmless? Men may not see the moral problem with porn, but they should begin to understand its psychological implications and the problem of these perceptions:

- ❖ An exaggerated view of sexual activity in society
- ❖ Diminished trust between intimate couples
- ❖ Belief that promiscuity is the natural state
- ❖ Belief that abstinence and sexual inactivity are unhealthy
- ❖ Cynicism about love and the need for personal affection
- ❖ Lack of interest in marriage and its sexual confinements
- ❖ Lack of attraction to having a family and raising children[37]

Porn is a fantasy that cannot achieve or replace true love and intimacy.

---

[37] Dolf Zillmann, "Influence of unrestrained access to erotica on adolescents' and young adults' dispositions toward sexuality," *Journal of Adolescent Health* 27 (Aug. 2000): 41–44.

TUG-OF-WAR

Have you ever watched a tug-of-war match? Unless one side is noticeably stronger than the other, tug-of-war battles are usually tedious and drawn out. One side yanks the other side inches forward, then that side counters and pulls back the other side by a few more inches. The match usually continues for some time, becoming a test of strength and endurance. Typically the side that is able to brace itself and withstand the constant back and forth—proving its durability over time—becomes the winner.

There is a constant tug-of-war in your brain related to pornography.

There are alterations in the prefrontal functioning of the brain that produce dysfunction regarding control and judgement. In everyday language this means one part of your brain is shouting "Yes! Do it!" while the more rational part of the brain resists, pulling back and saying, "No, not again!"[38]

---

[38] https://www.yourbrainonporn.com/rebooting-porn-use-faqs/does-porn-addiction-cause-irreversible-damage-to-the-brain/

Unfortunately, with addiction the rational part of the brain rarely outlasts the persistence of the prefrontal circuits in the brain. People usually "give in" to the cravings for more porn. It is what makes recovery from addiction very difficult.

When people are addicted to pornography their brains are completely rewired. Basic life functions such as acquiring food and water, nurturing relationships, creating stability in a job, and even engaging in sex all take a back seat to the addictive substance or behavior.[39]

Porn is persistent, gaining an unfair advantage in the relentless tug-of-war in your brain.

---

[39] https://www.theguardian.com/commentisfree/2013/sep/26/brain-scans-porn-addicts-sexual-tastes

THE NEW NORMAL

When we use a public restroom, we hope that it has been recently cleaned since so many people use the same restroom on a daily basis. That's not often the case, however, so there may be some restrooms we refuse to use because they are filthy.

What would happen, however, if our definition of what is clean shifted over time? We would have lower standards, so dirt and filth wouldn't be that bad. Mold growing in the corners? That would be perfectly understandable.

This is what happens to the brain when a person becomes addicted to pornography. The brain becomes desensitized.

Desensitization produces chemical and structural changes in the brain that actually make an individual less sensitive to pleasure. This is similar to tolerance, but it's not exactly the same thing.

When addicts become desensitized they don't just need more porn; they need more extreme versions of it. They don't simply crave more revolting material, they actually need it to get any type of pleasure. Shock and surprise jack up dopamine levels where they are comparable to a weightlifter shooting steroids to get amped for a workout. Thus the porn addict turns to more hardcore porn littered with strange and disturbing imagery.

This is why porn scenes of violence and rape are often idolized by viewers, representing some of the most popular types of porn on the web.

In a 2007 presentation, a group of doctors revealed that after analyzing 304 different porn scenes, they found 3,376 distinct acts of verbal or physical aggression. This equates to one act of aggression for every 90 seconds of porn viewing.[40]

> **Pornography misleads us into believing that violence and rape are actually acceptable in our society.**

[40] "Mapping the Pornographic Text: Content Analysis Research of Popular Pornography," Presentation by Robert Wosnitzer, Ana Bridges, and Michelle Chang at the National Feminist Antipornography Conference, Wheelock College, Boston, March 24, 2007.

A ROOM WITH NO DOORS

The user types in the URL for his favorite website and pulls up a video. The video has everything many men want: an attractive young woman exposing herself to the fantasy and imagination of the viewer.

But something is missing.

Why is it that looking at porn offers a rush of pleasure and thrill yet is followed by intense feelings of shame and guilt?

Pornography has been scientifically linked to loneliness and depression.[41] According to Dr. Gary R. Brooks, porn and depression will forever be associated because of the "pervasive disorder" it creates.

Among its most damaging symptoms is that pornography establishes an actual emotional barrier between humans. Porn users are often unable to relate to people of the opposite sex in an honest and

---

[41] Vincent Cyrus Yoder, Thomas B. Virden III, and Kiran Amin, "Internet Pornography and Loneliness: An Association?" *Sexual Addiction & Compulsivity* 12 (2005): 19–44.

intimate way, despite a *deep longing* for this personal affection.[42]

Have you ever tried breaking through a wall as opposed to using the door? It sounds difficult and painful. If you tried it, most people would assume you had lost your mind.

With pornography, however, the door is removed entirely and the individual has no choice but to break through walls in order to connect with others.

Porn users want to be held, touched, kissed, and loved but they are incapable of actively seeking these affections because pornography has corrupted their brains.

Pornography can lead to depression and loneliness, creating the opposite effect of what it promises to provide.

---

[42] Gary R. Brooks, *The Centerfold Syndrome: How Men Can Overcome Objectification and Achieve Intimacy with Women* (San Francisco: Jossy-Bass Publications, 1995).

ARTIFICIAL LOVE

Pornography attacks the reward center of the brain and greatly affects our ability to experience euphoria and pleasure.

The human brain is designed to produce thrill and excitement when tasks are completed. This is its natural function, but because porn artificially creates these thrills, the reward center is corrupted.

Many addictions (including alcohol, tobacco, opioids, and pornography) work drastically on the reward center.[43] Whether from a substance or a screen, they cause the secretion of intense amounts of dopamine (a chemical in the brain that produces euphoria), which initially feels very rewarding yet diminishes over time.

The diminishing reward is a result of tolerance. This unfortunate byproduct of addiction makes the user crave the substance more and more, yet over time the user receives less and less of a reward.

---

[43] https://www.theguardian.com/commentisfree/2013/sep/26/brain-scans-porn-addicts-sexual-tastes

The problem with tolerance is that it not only affects porn habits but also influences other parts of your life. Suddenly nothing really seems enjoyable. Things that you once loved doing without the aid of a screen now pale in comparison to the rush you get from looking at porn. Over time it feels like porn is the only aspect of your life that is satisfying, but in truth even that reward is diminishing.

> **Porn use hijacks the reward center of the brain.**

A TUNNEL WITH ONE ESCAPE

When does a hobby become an obsession? What is the first warning sign of addiction?

No matter how alluring pornography may be at first, it is *never* sustainable. One of the first red flags of addiction is when one *really* wants or craves an activity, yet after engaging in the behavior the user feels unfulfilled and the activity's pleasure diminishes.

Alcoholics will begin planning their days around when they can get their next drink. Similarly, one who is addicted to porn will begin planning his or her schedule around the next viewing. Pornography thus becomes the central focus of the addict's daily activities.

This aspect of addiction is defined as "sensitization."[44] This means that the brain circuits involved in motivation and reward seeking become hyper-sensitive to memories or cues associated with an addictive behavior. Consequently, pornographic images that were once enjoyed become less fulfilling.

---

[44] https://www.yourbrainonporn.com/rebooting-porn-use-faqs/does-porn-addiction-cause-irreversible-damage-to-the-brain/

Sensitizing cues can be anything from a simple act like turning on a computer to actually seeing a pop-up.

Pornography is like entering a tunnel with only one path— toward more porn.

AN AWFUL CYCLE

An alcoholic wakes up from a blackout drunk and desperately searches for a bottle, pleading for even a drop of liquor to reduce the shakes. The heroin addict is willing to break into a building and steal in order to get money for a fix, fearful of becoming dope sick.

While addiction to pornography may not have the visible extremes of drug abuse, it does contain some similarities when you examine its withdrawal effects.

Withdrawal from substance abuse is highly dangerous. Thousands of addicts are hospitalized every year because of severe withdrawal symptoms. Their brains have become so chemically dependent to a substance that when it is unexpectedly removed, their bodies and minds begins to react in an extremely negative way.

Though porn addiction does not have the same physical withdrawal effects, it does involve many of the same mental consequences.

People with addictions are known to return to the substance they abuse whenever they experience unpleasant feelings such as anxiety and depression.

Since pornography is already linked to depression and loneliness,[45] the unfortunate cycle is that abusers turn to porn when they are feeling down, yet pornography unconsciously leads to greater depression.

Addiction causes the brain to have dysfunctional stress circuits.[46] This means that even the tiniest ounce of stress can lead to relapse because the user believes the substance will provide immediate comfort.

But it doesn't.

Pornography, like other addictions, ultimately contributes to negative feelings rather than providing comfort for them.

This can be like betting on the worst team in a sports league. There is the thrill in betting on an underdog because you can get filthy rich if they pull the upset and win. Time and again they lose, however, which creates disappointment mixed with hope that *next* time will be different. But it never is.

Pornography fools you into thinking it will help you feel better, but over time it actually creates the opposite effect.

---

[45]   https://pdfs.semanticscholar.org/6111/5e99668a9f2b9da2db0e e5c066c1117a156b.pdf?_ga=2.161332025.529684032.1542623 458-1853466253.1542623458

[46]   http://www.psychguides.com/guides/porn-addiction/

A FAMILY DISEASE

Imagine a disease so contagious that it begins in you, then soon affects your spouse, children, and maybe even your co-workers and boss.

This happens all the time with alcoholism, which is known as "the family disease," but it also parallels what happens with a pornography addiction.

Pornography begins as something very isolated—it's done in hiding. After a while the retreat to conceal porn remains the same but other aspects of your behavior and activity begin to affect others. Your family starts to notice a difference.

Outside of alcoholism and drug addiction, there is no greater threat to family stability than pornography. An addiction to porn can create tense or strained relationships, dishonesty, disruptions to normal routines, and even an unsafe environment in the home.

Pornography deliberately intrudes on the personal confines of an intimate relationship. It impacts your relationship with a girlfriend, spouse, and children.

Not only are *you* impacted but also *their* attitude, intimacy, and overall well-being are affected.

An addiction to pornography, like alcoholism, is a "progressive disease." This means that it makes an individual's physical and mental health worse over time.

An incredible amount of damage is inflicted even though the average visitor to a pornographic website only spends 6.5 minutes per visit.[47] What other substance is that lethal in such a short amount of time?

Addiction to pornography is a progressive disease—it only gets worse over time.

---

[47] Bill Tancer, *Click: What Millions of People Are Doing Online and Why It Matters* (New York: Hyperion, 2008).

CHECKMATE

Have you ever played chess? It is amazing how in one moment a player can completely control a game (or at least feel like they are in control), then in an instant the other player calls out "Check . . . mate!"

In most instances, the eventual winner of a chess match is preparing for the final blow several moves in advance while the other player is oblivious. On other occasions, the soon-to-be defeated player is aware of impeding danger yet continues to be in denial. He or she assumes there's a way out, a way to block "checkmate."

The precise, calculated nature of addiction is similar to a chess match. Addiction does not take control over night, but when it does the effects are often abrupt, with a devastating, negative resolution.

Addiction is what many define as an "all-encompassing disease." It has a blistering, profound ability to take control of all aspects of one's life.

In most cases of addiction users do not initially notice any negative consequences from their actions. In fact, they experience the exact opposite, which leads them to abuse the substance or behavior more and more.

As time passes, however, the pieces on the gameboard move. The addiction starts to gain an unfair advantage. Addiction strongly influences and adversely affects:[48]

❖ **Relationships** — Pornography addiction is not singular. The user may consider it an isolated, harmless activity yet an addiction to porn leads to tension and stress with a significant other, friends, family, co-workers, and supervisors. Of all the negative consequences of porn addiction, relationships are generally the most severely impacted.[49]

❖ **Finances** — While porn is more abundant and free than ever, porn addiction still contributes to financial problems. Sometimes they are obvious like the cost of a monthly subscription to an adult website. In most cases, finances are affected by indirect means such as consistent tardiness to work, poor work performance, a divorce or separation that leads to financial turmoil, or termination from a job because of porn use.[50]

❖ **Physical/Mental health** — Drug addiction may cause more apparent physical side effects, but pornography also has negative implications on your health, particularly your mental health.

---

[48] https://novarecoverycenter.com/treatment-programs/behavioral-therapies/consequences-drug-use/
[49] http://www.tylerstillman.info/uploads/2/1/5/2/21520198/_a_love_that_doesnt_last_lambert_et_al.pdf. Also, https://www.psychguides.com/guides/porn-addiction/
   And: https://journals.sagepub.com/doi/abs/10.3149/jms.2201.64
[50] https://www.ncbi.nlm.nih.gov/pubmed/23167900

Porn use contributes to isolation, loneliness, and depression because it directly affects the chemical makeup of your brain.[51]

❖ **Legal matters** — Studies show that pornography leads to people being desensitized to rape and other violent sexual crimes. This is not only a personal problem but also a societal concern since our legal system tends to be lenient in punishing these types of crimes. Furthermore, porn addiction can lead to individual legal problems, including the financial and emotional costs of divorce or child support.[52]

❖ **Personal character** — Among the least addressed negative consequences of addiction is its attack on personal character. Addicts are known for losing their self-identity and dignity. They are suffocated by shame and guilt. Honest, dependable people become pathological liars who are irresponsible. Addiction changes a person's morals, values, perceptions, and, in extreme cases, their complete identity and personality.[53]

How do you buck the trend? How do you avoid the fatal "checkmate" from porn?

Studies indicate that maintaining positive expectations of porn (when someone romanticizes the behavior) contributes to a higher likelihood of relapse.

[51] https://fightthenewdrug.org/porn-can-make-you-more-depressed-and-lonely/. Also, https://pdfs.semanticscholar.org/
[52] http://www.drjudithreisman.com/archives/Senate-Testimony-20041118_Weaver.pdf
[53] https://fightthenewdrug.org/problem-porn-shame/

To avoid this kind of false romanticism, people must maintain an awareness of porn's negative consequences through a supportive, community-based environment.

In the end, most victims of porn addiction realize that the negative consequences vastly outweigh any potential benefits.

Pornography negatively impacts you relationally, physically, mentally, financially, and legally.

STRENGTH

He gives strength to the weary and increases the power of the weak.
(ISAIAH 40:29)

LIKE A LION

If pornography was advertised like a commercial for a prescription medication, it would first mention the benefits followed by a long list of side effects. The end of the commercial could sound like this:

"Pornography may cause intense emotions of shame, guilt, regret, condemnation, and remorse. Patients have reported extreme cases of anxiety, worry, depression, isolation, and feelings of loneliness. Men will have a reduced interest in real women. Sexual arousal and intimacy may be difficult. Do not use pornography unless you want to experience life exactly the opposite of how God intended it."

Though it may sound humorous, this is exactly what happens to an individual hooked on porn.

Shame is a person's feeling that something is fundamentally wrong with him or her. As defined, shame actually causes pain, especially mentally as the person is "humiliated or distressed."

Feeling ashamed can lead to self-hatred or low

self-esteem.[54] These negative feelings are compounded by the fact that shame and guilt causes a person to retreat (go into hiding), much like Adam and Eve did after they ate the forbidden fruit. Instead of addressing God or others about the issue and asking for help, the person withdraws back into shame and silence.

All the negative consequences of pornography and addiction are fundamentally rooted in shame. Shame is a problem because the person feels so humiliated and distressed about the behavior that it sabotages their strength, leaving them paralyzed. Rarely do they take a positive course of action.

First Peter 5:8 reminds us that "the devil prowls around like a roaring lion looking for someone to devour." The enemy is not simply trying to trick and seduce you with porn; ultimately he wants to *devour* you—heart, mind, soul, and strength.

> **Pornography is a savage beast that doesn't relent until it has devoured all your strength.**

---

[54] Jon Mooallem, "A Disciplined Business," *The New York Times Magazine*, April 29, 2007. https://www.nytimes.com/2007/04/29/magazine/29kink.t.html (accessed Dec. 27, 2012).

TROPHY ON A WALL

Hunters have a tradition of displaying the mounted heads of prized game they kill. These trophies signify their pride in the animal they tracked, killed, and dragged from the wilderness.

Pornography has helped to foster a culture that treats women like hunted prey—animals to be tracked and displayed, much to the pleasure of the waiting audience.

This is not only unfair to women, but also disregards God's design—He made men *and* women in His image, after His likeness.[55]

We live in a culture that celebrates "trophyism," which is the idea that beautiful women are collectibles—they show the world who a man really is. This mindset creates a variety of delusions, including:

❖ Objectification — the attitude that women are not human beings, but are objects to be rated by size and shape

---

[55] See Genesis 1:26

- ❖ Validation — the need to prove one's masculinity by being with a "dream girl" or creating other misconceptions of beauty
- ❖ Fear of True Intimacy — the inability to relate to women in reality where honesty and affection are desirable

---

Pornography weakens a man's ability to love and to be attracted to a woman in a realistic manner.

CLONING A GENERATION OF SUCKERS

When men and women are asked what they consider to be some of the benefits of watching porn, aside from the obvious ("it makes me feel good," "it's a release and an escape"), people falsely believe porn makes them better lovers.

In reality, pornography presents a remarkably jaded and incorrect version of sexual encounters. It teaches men that foreplay is unnecessary, that females only enjoy rough sex, that intercourse lasts for hours, and that women enjoy being objectified and treated as inferior beings.[56]

Porn basically distorts *everything* that is real related to sex and intimacy.

Older people may recognize the distortions and be even more attracted to porn because of the fantasy

---

[56] https://www.dailydot.com/via/debunking-sex-myths-learned -porn/, https://www.salon.com/2014/01/06/10_ways_porn_perpet uates_myths_about_men_partner/

these myths create. For younger audiences, however, this distortion actually causes them to believe this is how people "get it on." For many young people, porn is the new method of sex education.

No one likes being considered a "sucker." This term suggests that the person is naïve, gullible, ignorant, and clueless. It's never been popular to be a sucker, so why is it popular to think of pornography as sex education?

Sadly, many Millennials don't know any different because porn is the only sex education they have received. Thus when they eventually seek to experience real love, sex, and intimacy they have long been swayed by porn's misconceptions.

In his best-selling book *Wild at Heart*, John Eldredge concludes:

> "What makes pornography so addictive is that more than anything else in a lost man's life, it makes him feel like a man without ever requiring a thing of him. The less a guy feels like a real man in the presence of a real woman, the more vulnerable he is to porn. This is every man's deepest fear: to be exposed, to be found out, to be discovered as an impostor, and not really a man."

Pornography clones a generation of suckers who believe it is legitimate sex education and actually makes them better lovers.

SUCKING OUT THE LIFE

Cancer is one of the most feared diseases because of its rapid growth. It starts with a single cell, which is somehow altered and then begins to multiply out of control. A cluster of such abnormal cells creates a tumor, and from there the disease can really become destructive.

Pornography and cancer share several similarities.

The two begin small. Just like a cell is only visible under a microscope, the first time a man looks at porn may seem insignificant; a tiny little detail. But what happens when it starts to grow?

Malignant tumors are the most catastrophic as they overcrowd and push out healthy cells, causing interference with central bodily functions and drawing out nutrients. Tumors literally suck the life out of a human body.

Like cancer, the effects of pornography spread across the body, slowly altering and corroding its core. First it impacts the body, then the heart and mind, and eventually the soul. The cancerous decay caused by porn can be swift and extensive, but it doesn't have to be permanent.

Did you know that not all tumors in the body are cancerous? Even when they are, a variety of treatments exist that can send the cancer into remission. Yet treatment is only available to those who seek help.

The cancer of pornography is no different. Its impact on the body *is* reversible. The detrimental effects *are* treatable, which means the body can be restored to function as God intended it.

Like a cancer, pornography attacks and destroys an individual's strength and results in a vulnerable heart, mind, and soul.

OVERCOMING OBSTACLES

*"When you come upon a wall, throw
your hat over it. Then go get your hat."*
- IRISH PROVERB

The path of life is littered with barriers and obstacles. Sometimes these are manageable and we navigate them with ease. On other occasions, they appear massive and unconquerable. Thus we may divert from our intended path in order to avoid these obstructions.

Pornography is one of the single biggest obstacles to a healthy marriage.

According to sociologist Jill Manning, research indicates that the consumption of pornography is associated with three destructive trends:

❖ Increased marital distress that may lead to separation or divorce
❖ Decreased marital intimacy and sexual satisfaction

❖ Devaluation of monogamy, marriage, and child rearing[57]

In cases of divorce, a separate report[58] added that 68 percent of divorces involved one party meeting a new lover over the internet and 56 percent involved one party having "an obsessive interest in pornographic websites."

The report added that porn left partners with feelings of "hurt, betrayal, rejection, abandonment, loneliness, isolation, humiliation, jealousy and anger." Partners added that cyber affairs were as emotionally painful as offline affairs.

Pornography says that it's okay to look at naked bodies online—it's only a fantasy where no one is harmed in the process. But pornography knows all the tricks. It is perfectly fine with establishing obstacles so enormous that partners become content with the barrier it creates for true intimacy.

The lesson taught in the Irish proverb about a man who approaches a wall and flings over his hat is an important one. The man acknowledges the barrier and

---

[57] Jill Manning, "Hearing on pornography's impact on marriage & the family," U.S. Senate Hearing: Subcommittee on the Constitution, Civil Rights and Property Rights, Committee on Judiciary, Nov. 10, 2005. http://www.judiciary.senate.gov/hearings/testimony.cfm?id=e655f9e2809e5476862f735da10c87dc&wit_id=e-655f9e2809e5476862f735da10c87dc-1-3 (accessed Dec. 27, 2012).

[58] Jonathan Dedmon, "Is the Internet bad for your marriage? Online affairs, pornographic sites playing greater role in divorces." Press Release from The Dilenschneider Group, Inc., Nov. 14, 2002. http://www.prnewswire.com/news-releases/is-the-internet-bad-for-your-marriage-online-affairs-pornographic-sites-playing-greater-role-in-divorces-76826727.html (accessed Dec. 27, 2012).

commits to overcoming it by first tossing over one of his possessions. Then, if he wants to get his hat back, he must overcome the obstacle.

The proverb is also symbolic of recovery from any addiction. It is rarely easy, but can be overcome if one is willing to commit fully, first by surrendering a part of his body, after which the rest can follow.

> **Pornography is perhaps the single biggest obstacle to a healthy, thriving marriage.**

IS THE GRASS GREENER?

You may realize pornography is popular online, but did you know that porn websites receive more traffic each month than Amazon, Netflix, and Twitter *combined*?[59]

The high-volume traffic of porn sites may not be all that shocking, but the way users appear to praise and even worship easy access to online pornography is most definitely disturbing.

Individuals who are "repeatedly exposed to pornography begin to compare the whole fantasy experience to their sex lives. Instead of being drawn to one woman or one man, the individual ends up being turned on by the variety and novelty porn offers."[60]

Neurobiologist Peter Milner supports this theory because our brains are wired to be attracted to that which is unfamiliar and novel. He explains that this

---

[59] https://www.huffingtonpost.com/2013/05/03/internet-porn-stats_n_3187682.html
[60] Judith Reisman, "The Impotence Pandemic," *WorldNetDaily*, September 27, 2007. https://www.wnd.com/2007/09/43723/

inward drive is what enables us to discover and learn new things as well as to adapt to our environment.

Milner concludes that it is very possible to "become addicted to novelty and uncertainty," thus porn might be considered by some to be the perfect remedy.

The familiar face and body of a spouse no longer arouses the partner like it once did. Consequently, the partner turns to the novelty of pornography. This is the classic "grass is always greener on the other side" mindset. The problem is that it's an illusion.

Porn trains a person to retreat to the realm of fantasy in order to feel aroused.

FRITTER & WASTE

The clock goes tick tock.

In the 21st century we have the rare ability to control just about every aspect of our lives to the finest detail. Video games are paused whenever we get a phone call or crave a snack. Netflix provides on-demand services where we pick and choose, watching and pausing at will.

Still, there is one aspect of our lives that we cannot control, and never will control: time.

Christians learn that we only get one life on earth. When compared to eternity our earthly lives are extraordinarily short.

A common theme among those who struggle with pornography is their frustration about the time they have wasted.

In the moment, things may feel familiar and grand but after looking at porn the individual often experiences the emotions of self-loathing and self-hatred.

You could reason that nothing good comes from something that causes you to feel guilty and shameful about it after the fact. You could also reason that nothing good is done in hiding. Pornography is a master at both, and it skillfully robs you of your precious time!

Are you tired of squandering a life consumed by porn? Do you feel like your time—your life—has been wasted?

Porn is a distraction hell-bent on wasting your sacred time, which you can never recover after it's gone.

THE DISTRACTED WORKER

Have you ever noticed that the longer you work the more difficult it is to focus? When it's late in the work day it seems like no matter how hard you try to stay motivated, something mentally exhausts you just like a runner in a marathon who has reached the brink and can't move, not even one more step.

Pornography directly attacks your productivity. It creates a permanent roadblock that most of the time leaves you feeling like an exhausted and emotionally drained runner.

Statistics prove that porn is a major distraction in work environments, and some people have even lost their jobs after getting caught viewing porn while on the job.

The number of Christian men viewing pornography at work virtually mirrors the national average. More than half of Christian men admitted to viewing pornography on the job at least once in the previous three months. Christian men between the ages of 31–49 are especially vulnerable.[61]

---

[61] Proven Men Porn Survey (conducted by Barna Group) https://www.provenmen.org/2014PornSurvey/

Psychologists who specialize in studying work environments tend to agree that productivity and efficiency are lacking at current workspaces for a number of reasons, though the most significant contribution is the sheer amount of information we process these days and the number of distractions we face.[62]

According to another study, some individuals report problems during and after viewing pornography, such as missing sleep or forgetting important appointments.[63] These factors contribute to poor work performance, even if you don't view porn on the job.

> **Porn not only has a negative impact on personal relationships, but also on performance at work.**

[62] https://www.psychologytoday.com/us/blog/your-brain-work/200910/easily-distracted-why-its-hard-focus-and-what-do-about-it
[63] https://www.ncbi.nlm.nih.gov/pubmed/23167900

ISOLATION DEVASTATION

Clint Eastwood made a fortune by frequently representing the strong, silent type who preferred to "go it alone" and consistently overcame nearly insurmountable odds. He is one of many Hollywood "heroes" who were able to tackle armies of enemies alone. These characters are depicted as strong, brave, invincible, and fearless. They are presented as *real* men.

The problem with this characterization is that it's highly influential yet rarely effective in the real world. Men were never intended to go it alone without any help. God makes it perfectly clear that the church is designed as a place of fellowship, where men (not just women) gather with other men to get real about their issues and to find help in dealing with those concerns.

Individuals in recovery, regardless of the addiction, will quickly attest to the value of community because they know that without it their recovery is nearly impossible.

The reason so many addicts relapse time and time again is because they seek help from others for a short time, but then mistakenly believe they have been cured and can leave the confines of a caring community. Thus they again become isolated, which is a prime predictor of relapse.

The Big Book of Alcoholics Anonymous warns that isolation contributes to the ideal that an addict can "play God." This is portrayed in the image of Clint Eastwood marching down a Main Street in the Old West, alone with guns blazing. No man (or even a group of men) is a viable match for him.

In reality this concept is absurd. The single gunslinger would be dropped in a matter of seconds from a collective (whether of lawmen or outlaws) mounting a resistance. Isolation would contribute to the person's downfall.

The same is true for an isolated addict.

But what if the numbers were balanced to reflect a fair fight?

Ecclesiastes 4:12 emphasizes, "Though one may be overpowered, two can defend themselves. A cord of three strands is not quickly broken." Recovery from an addiction to pornography is possible only with a caring, supportive community.

It's nearly impossible to overcome porn addiction without other soldiers who have also struggled in the battle.

WALKING IN CIRCLES

Have you ever set out on a hike after dark with a flash-light? The surrounding territory is masked in uncertainty. There could be predators lurking just beyond the light. But if you stay focused on the path, with the light pointed ahead, you will eventually reach your destination.

What happens, though, when halfway through your journey the batteries get weak and the light begins to diminish? How about when the light goes out completely?

It can be frightening walking in complete darkness, right?

Living a life that is influenced by pornography is like hiking without a flashlight. You may have a sense of where the path is, but the going is difficult because you can't see the full picture.

Pornography disrupts the plan God has for your life. This is confirmed by countless testimonies from those who lost a spouse, a family, or a job to porn. They have suffered irreversible actions that left perma-nent scars and caused much internal turmoil, regret, and self-condemnation.

It may start by staying up later and later at night to feed a porn habit. That's the only time of the day you are able to sneak away. While it might seem like an innocent pastime, as you consume more porn it begins to impact your sleeping schedule. Thus you awake feeling groggy and unfocused. This carries over to your job, where at first just your work performance suffers but later you also have trouble getting to work on time because you keep hitting snooze on your alarm.

Proverbs 16:9 emphasizes, "The heart of man plans his way, but the Lord *establishes his steps.*" (emphasis added) Likewise Proverbs 3:5-6 instructs, "Trust in the Lord with all your heart, and do not lean on your own understanding. In all your ways acknowledge him, and he will *make straight your paths.* (emphasis added)

When you turn to porn you essentially walk a path that goes in circles. The troubling cycle repeats itself again and again. Things you once cared about are negatively affected as you try to navigate the darkened path of pornography.

"For I know the plans I have for you, declares the Lord, plans for welfare and not for evil, to give you a future and a hope."[64]

> **Pornography disorients Christians on the path God has planned for their lives.**

---

[64] Jeremiah 29:11

EPILOGUE

Angry. Distracted. Guilty. Shamed. Distant. Empty.

If words like these describe how you feel because of your regular viewing of pornography, you're not alone. And while viewing porn may drive a wedge between you and God, you're not the first person to find that a sexually charged sin leads you to a dark place.

Some of the greatest figures in the Bible made historically bad decisions. Two of the most famous in the Old Testament—Solomon and David—each suffered mightily with lust. And they weren't alone. In fact, when the Apostle Paul wrote in 1 Timothy 1:15, "Christ Jesus came into the world to save sinners—of whom I am the worst"—the expression struck a chord with countless believers who find themselves wrestling with sins of all types.

Porn has transformed into an evil empire. It takes no prisoners. Its ulterior motive is to radically convert your body, heart, mind, and soul. It is damaging yet not irreversible.

Does porn use have you living in the dumps right

now? Do you feel like your life has been destroyed by
guilt and shame?

God wants to remove that awful junk from your
mind and restore your soul. He seeks to break you free
from the chains and shackles of sin (Luke 8:29) and
remove the yoke of slavery (Galatians 5:1).

1. No sin is too extreme for God.

"When you were dead in your sins and in the
uncircumcision of your flesh, God made you
alive with Christ. He forgave us all our sins. . .
. He has taken it away, nailing it to the cross."
- COLOSSIANS *2:13-14*

Perhaps you are struggling to come clean regarding
your dependence on porn because you think no one
will understand. You think God does not understand,
but this is simply not true. Jesus Christ came to earth to
die for the sins of mankind. Acts 3:19 reminds us that
all sin is "wiped out" when we repent and come clean.

2. Sin will try to keep you isolated.

"If we confess our sins, he is faithful
and just and will forgive us our sins and
purify us from all unrighteousness."
- 1 JOHN *1:9*

Pride will tell you that you've got this; that your individual circumstances are not all that horrible; that
everyone is doing it. Pride seeks to keep you isolated,
which is exactly where the Enemy wants to contain
believers. It is his only play at this point. When we

confess and seek help from others, change can and most certainly will occur in countless lives.

3. There is no condemnation in your past.

> *"Therefore, there is now no condemnation*
> *for those who are in Christ Jesus."*
> *- ROMANS 8:1*

You may feel guilty about your past, and shame may consume your thoughts. Yet God makes it clear that you are not to live in condemnation. We are still sinners after we give our life to God, and all fall short of perfection. The question is how do you move forward—what are you going to dedicate your time and energy to in the future?

4. God loves sinners of all types.

> *"Perseverance, character; and character*
> *hope. And hope does not put us to shame,*
> *because God's love has been poured*
> *out into our hearts through the Holy*
> *Spirit, who has been given to us."*
> *- ROMANS 5:4-5*

Perhaps you've heard many times before that God loves you, but have you ever really felt it? Maybe you did at first, when you acknowledged Christ as your Lord and Savior, yet that feeling has faded over time. You feel undeserving of His love because of your past with porn, but no sin ever changes God's love for you. Everything is recoverable. Psalms 103:10-12 reminds us that we are not treated as "our sins deserve."

5. No longer a yoke.

> *"For freedom Christ has set us free;*
> *stand firm therefore, and do not*
> *submit again to a yoke of slavery."*
> *- GALATIANS 5:1*

The term *yoke* is used often in the Bible but tends to get overlooked in the modern Western world. A yoke is a wooden crosspiece that is fastened over the necks of two animals and then attached to a plow or cart. It is essentially complete bondage.

In the Bible, a yoke is symbolic of sin and addiction, two issues that perplexed mankind in the ancient world and still do to the present day.

One of the most powerful verses found in the New Testament for those who feel down, disgusted, guilty, and ashamed about their past transgressions is found in Galatians 5, which reminds believers that they've been set free from sin.

You can be free from porn. Yes, it is a powerful tool the enemy wants to use against you, yet your faith in Christ Jesus is far stronger. When you confess your sins, cast away guilt and shame, fellowship with others, and rediscover the love Jesus has for you—healing can officially begin.

What will you do to get started on a new path?

DISCUSSION GUIDE

Use this four-week discussion guide with a friend, small group, or Sunday school class to bring this conversation into the light. Honest conversations are very powerful in helping to reshape perspective, offer encouragement, and bring healing.

WEEK ONE: HEART
Read pages 1–25

Ice Breaker: TOP OF MIND

❖ Pass around a pad of sticky notes and a pen/ pencil to each group participant. Have each person take a blank sheet.

❖ Ask each person to write down a one-word answer to this question:

✚ What is the first thing you think of when you hear the word *"pornography?"*

❖ Have each person share their word and briefly explain or elaborate on why they chose that word.

Discussion/Study Questions:

1. In what ways would you say pornography "poisons" the human heart?

2. Would you say pornography has any legitimate role in our society?

3. Does pornography provide a fraudulent emotional or spiritual fulfillment of a legitimate desire? If so, explain how?

4. Would you consider pornography to be a type of idolatry? If so, how would you say the human

heart participates and worships pornography illegitimately?

Application:

❖ **MEMORIZE:** Proverbs 4:23 this week

> *"Above all else, guard your heart,*
> *for everything you do flows from it."*
> *– PROVERBS 4:23*

❖ **PRAY:** Ask God how He wants to challenge or change your thinking regarding pornography and how it affects His people.

❖ **OPEN UP:** Tell a close friend about this study on pornography and how God is challenging your views about it. Ask them what they believe God thinks about pornography and its presence in our culture.

WEEK TWO: SOUL
Read pages 27–47

Ice Breaker: AIRPLANE THOUGHTS

- ❖ Give each person in the group a 3" x 5" card and a pen/pencil.
- ❖ Set the stage: You're on an airplane in the window seat of a three-seat row. On your immediate right is a person of the opposite sex. On the outside aisle seat is a person of the same sex. After the plane takes off, the person in the middle seat opens their iPad or tablet and starts viewing pornography freely.
- ❖ On one side of the card, describe your feelings toward the person viewing the pornography. On the other side of the card, describe your feelings toward the person in the aisle seat. Keep your answers to 15 words or less.
- ❖ Have each person in the group:
  - ✛ Share their answers and briefly explain or elaborate on their feelings.
  - ✛ Explain what they would *do or say,* if anything.

Discussion/Study Questions:

1. Why do you think Jesus compares merely *"looking at a woman lustfully"* to adultery?
2. How would you say viewing porn affects a person's prayer life?
3. What would you think or do if you found out the pastor of your own church viewed pornography?
4. Pornography use typically induces both *shame* and *guilt*. How would you describe the difference between these two emotional responses?

Application:

❖ **MEMORIZE:** Matthew 16:26 this week:

"What good will it be for someone to gain the whole world, yet forfeit their soul? Or what can anyone give in exchange for their soul?"
—MATTHEW 16:26

❖ **PRAY:** Ask God to give you insight about how He wants you to act toward others who use or are struggling with pornography.

❖ **OPEN UP:** Tell a trusted friend about the first time you became aware of or viewed pornography yourself and how it made you feel.

WEEK THREE: MIND
Read pages 49–73

Ice Breaker: TSA CHECKPOINT

- ❖ Give each person in the group a 3" x 5" card and a pen/pencil.
- ❖ Ask each person to make a list of five things that you CANNOT bring on an airplane on one side of the card.
- ❖ Have each person in the group share their list and describe WHY each item is not allowed.
- ❖ On the reverse side of the card, have each person write five things they *don't* or *won't* allow into their own minds because they are deemed unsafe or unhealthy.
- ❖ Have each person share their list and describe WHY they stop these things at the TSA checkpoint of their mind.

Discussion/Study Questions:

1. What would you say are some of the *real, negative consequences* a person might experience because of viewing pornography?

2. How would you say viewing porn over time desensitizes a person's thinking about sex?

3. How would you say an addiction to pornography could actually become deadly like an addiction to alcohol or heroin?

4. Paul encourages us in Philippians 4:8, "*Whatever is true, whatever is noble, whatever is right, whatever is pure, whatever is lovely, whatever is admirable—if anything is excellent or praiseworthy—think about such things.*" Would you say any kind of pornography falls into one of these categories?

Application:

❖ **MEMORIZE:** Romans 12:2 this week:

"Do not conform to the pattern of this world, but be transformed by the renewing of your mind. Then you will be able to test and approve what God's will is—his good, pleasing and perfect will."
—ROMANS 12:2

❖ **PRAY:** Ask God to convict you about anything negative you've been allowing into your mind and to show you how they may be negatively impacting your life.

❖ **OPEN UP:** Tell a trusted friend about a negative thought pattern you sometime have or struggle with that is bothersome or that makes you feel guilt or shame.

WEEK FOUR: STRENGTH
Read pages 75–95

Ice Breaker: COFFEE SHOP SURPRISE

- ❖ Set the stage: You're having coffee in a local coffee shop when you suddenly notice a friend from church across the room sitting at a table alone, drinking coffee, and viewing their smartphone. You walk up behind them to say hello and before they see you, you notice they are viewing pornography on their phone.
- ❖ Have each person in the group answer the following:
  - ✛ What do you immediately "feel"?
  - ✛ What will you *do* or *not do* once you've become aware of the porn?
  - ✛ What will you think about the person later that night or the next day when you are alone?

Discussion/Study Questions:

1. How would you describe what shame feels like?
2. How would you say pornography objectifies women?

3. How does pornography violate loyalty in the context of marriage?
4. How is viewing pornography a failure to love the Lord you God with all one's *strength*?

Application:

❖ **MEMORIZE:** Isaiah 40:29 this week:

> *"He gives strength to the weary and increases the power of the weak."*
> *– ISAIAH 40:29*

❖ **PRAY:** Ask God to reveal areas of your relationship with Him that need to be strengthened.

❖ **OPEN UP:** Be honest with a friend or family member about an area in your life where you feel emotionally or spiritually "weak."

RESOURCES

NEED HELP?

Below is a list and links to some resources that help people struggling with pornography, sexual addictions, and behaviors. Of course, your local church should be able to provide assistance, give recommendations, or have programs of their own. If you're struggling with an addiction or have a behavior you can't control or stop, we believe these resources can help steer you in the right direction toward healing and recovery.

RECOVERY GROUPS & PROGRAMS:

Celebrate Recovery
Celebrate Recovery is a Christ-centered, twelve-step recovery program for anyone struggling with hurt, pain, or addiction of any kind. Celebrate Recovery is a safe place to find community and freedom from the issues that are controlling our life.

celebraterecovery.com

Sexaholics Anonymous

A fellowship with a solution to the problems of lust, sex, and pornography addiction.

www.sa.org

BOOKS

- ❖ Covenant Eyes. *Your Brain on Porn*. 2019. Download the free ebook here: http://bit.ly/YourBrainOnPornFreeBook.
- ❖ Arterburn, S., Stoeker, F., and Yorkey, M. *Every Young Man's Battle*. Colorado Springs: WaterBrook Press, 2010.
- ❖ Arterburn, S. and Martinkus, J. *Worthy of Her Trust*. Colorado Springs: WaterBrook Press, 2014.
- ❖ Gallagher, S. *At the Altar of Sexual Idolatry*. Dry Ridge, Kentucky: Pure Life Ministries, 2016.
- ❖ Gross, C. and Luff, S. *Pure Eyes*. Grand Rapids: Baker Books, 2010.
- ❖ Weiss, D. *Clean*. Nashville: Thomas Nelson, 2013.

CONFERENCES & WORKSHOPS

Every Man's Battle Conferences
Porn. Lust. Affairs. They've taken your life to a place you never could have imagined. It's a serious problem that requires a serious solution. *Every Man's Battle* is the place where men engage in the battle to restore their sexual integrity. In this intensive three-day workshop, you'll work with licensed Christian counselors who will arm you with the weapons you need for victory. The enemy may have wounded you, but the battle is not over. Register today. Too much is at stake not to take action.

https://newlife.com/workshops/every-mans-battle/

ONLINE RESOURCES

XXX Church
Porn addiction is one of the most difficult addictions to overcome, but XXX Church is your online resource for pornography addiction help. We prevail over sex and porn addiction through awareness, prevention, and recovery.

https://www.xxxchurch.com/

PROVEN MEN
Our mission is to see **Proven Men** *walking the* **Proven Path** within **Proven Churches.** We have a passion to see men being set free from their sin and passionately pursuing Jesus in a personal relationship with Him. We desire to see this transformation and growth happen within the walls of the local church! It's all about men experiencing the power of the gospel within their lives and struggles!

https://www.provenmen.org/

TRUEFACE

Here at Trueface, we want to help you increase your influence by trusting God and others with yourself. We offer a variety of means for your journey, including books, study guides, events, videos, podcasts, group online education, consulting, and partnerships. In this relational process of building trust, we believe you will discover the true face of Jesus, again—maybe for the first time. He is the Source of every high-trust community of grace.

http://www.trueface.org/

PURE LIFE MINISTRIES

Pure Life has been a pioneer in dealing with sexual addiction and its consequences for thirty years now. During that time, thousands of people have found freedom through our counseling programs and teaching materials.

https://www.purelifeministries.org/

INTERNET FILTERS AND ACCOUNTABILITY SOFTWARE

Covenant Eyes
https://www.covenanteyes.com

X3 Watch
https://x3watch.com

Net Nanny
http://www.netnanny.com/

Truple (Android)
http://www.truple.io

Made in the USA
San Bernardino, CA
25 March 2019